Adrift in Verse

By
Becky Coelho

Adrift in Verse

Other works by Becky Coelho

"Born In December" © 2006
"Through The Crystal" © 2007
"It Doesn't Always Show On The Outside" © 2009
"Building Dominoes" © 2009
"Secret of Mill Creek Raceway" © 2009

ISBN: 978-0-557-74847-1

Cover Art: "Sunspots II" by Sherri Lemire

Printed by: Lulu.com

A special thanks to all my English Teachers

Contents

Nature

Falling Stars

If wishes were stars my sky would never be dark
They fly across the sky finding a place to rest
Many have fallen …

If dreams were stars my sky would never be dark
They lighten the darkness of my sleep
Many have burnt out…

If hopes were stars my sky would never be dark
They are the stepping stones on which we walk
Many have sunk….

If prayers were stars my sky would never be dark
They ride their way to Heaven
Many are left unanswered…

If love were stars my sky would never be dark
They fly to the hearts of all
Many never return…

But stars are but sparkles in a midnight sky
Dreams, a result of sleep
My hopes are wishes of things to be if
Prayers are left unsaid

If wishes, dreams and prayers were stars
There would be no darkness in my life
And love is something I must give myself
Before giving it away

Cold Sunshine

The winter ground is still frozen
A chill is in the air
But the rays from the winter sun
Takes away each care

The ice still floats upon the lake
It glitters for all to see
It is at this moment in time
That I truly feel free

The geese are playing their happy tune
In a small inlet bay
They flap their wings and splatter the air
What are they trying to say?

Long shadows fall across the lake
The trees sway in the breeze
The branches look so naked now
They have lost their Autumn leaves

But the sunshine promises new beginnings
All across the earth
And Spring will be here very soon
A time for its rebirth

I sit and look across the lake
And wonder what will be
Just wait a few more weeks, I think
And it will be ours for free

Cardinals

This morning as I passed by the window
Something strange caught my eye
A flash of red, another too
Against the winter sky

I stopped, turned and pulled back the drape
And all I could do was stare
Five little cardinals, three dads and two moms
Were happily playing out there

They danced on the lawn
Now covered with snow
They were singing so sweetly
As if giving a show

I watched them a while
Before the flew away
Flying by me they promised
To come back another day

Outside My Window

Butterflies and hummingbirds
Outside my window play
I hope to catch a glimpse of them
Sometimes I sit all day

The butterflies, so vivid and bright
Skip among the flowers
They play and dance upon the leaves
Sometimes they stay for hours

The hummingbirds fly so still
It seems not a move they make
Then they land upon the perch
For the sweet nectar they partake

Hummingbirds and butterflies
Around my house they fly
They come so I can watch them play
Or is it me upon which they spy?

Snow

The light through my morning window
Blinded my still sleepy eyes
The sun was glistening off the new fallen snow
And on each snowflake as it flies

The quiet was so deafening
I truly thought I had died
But then I heard a cardinal sing
And dared to look outside

The waves of snow rolled over the fields
Near the barn there was a big drift
The air was cold and bit at my face
The clouds were moving so swift

It's been days since that morning snowfall
And we hear the ice crunch under our feet
The blanket of snow is all rumpled now
And it's stained and not so neat

It's times like this that I make a wish
For either spring to come real soon
Or to have another snowfall
Beneath the light of a winter's moon

Summer Rain

The clouds hung lightly on the trees near the bluff
The leaves were white with its fuzz
The rain has passed and now it is cool
The sky is lighter than it was

Droplets cling to the upturned leaves
They are grateful for the drink
Fresh and clean from a late summer shower
Lilies sway as the Black-eyed Susans wink

Given a break for just a brief time
From the heat and the glaring sun
Birds sing as they splash in the puddles
Oh, they're having so much fun

The storm is gone, the clouds move out
The sun shines so far above
All is well, new life begins
Because of God's plan of love.

The Flower

I am amazed at the cold gray steel
Of buildings standing so tall
The shape and size are overwhelming
They make me feel so small

Each building rises higher than the other
And they all block out the sun's light
When down on the street through cold cement
A small flower begins his fight

He pushes through a crack in the sidewalk
A struggle to begin to grow
With time and effort he could become
A colorful daisy giving a show

People stop along their way
Knowing what he needs
Some sprinkle drops of water
Hoping there are other seeds

Grow strong and tall young daisy
Let your roots take hold in the ground
For when people see your flowers
Smiles will be passed around

If one can grow so tall and lovely
In this world so harsh and gray
There is hope for me in this big world
To find my way some day

The Lonesome Moon

The full yellow moon grabbed for the clouds
Pleading to them not to let him fall
But the clouds rushed by on their merry way
And the thunder roared its mighty laugh.

The moon was shadowed by the rolling dark clouds
While the stars twinkled in clusters
The moon was content to be alone
in a dark and cloudy sky.

But hoping just one time
to shine above all the rest,
Gradually he sunk below the earth
letting the sun take over the sky.

Challenge Poems

The Gardener

While walking along the promenade
His mutism was yelling in a tenor voice
His endless monologue seemed merciless
I have to affirm, it was my choice

I felt like a snoop or a hidden hare
Reading his touch of each small seed
Inducting them in discount china pots
His loyal conservation was all they need

With daily frequency I would watch
Him checking to see if they grow
We'll wile away the time until
The luxurious flowers show

Challenge Words ~ Poem #1

1. promenade 2. Mutism 3. Hare 4. Discount 5. China 6. Reading 7. Tenor 8. Monologue 9. Luxurious 10. Frequency 11. Seed 12. Endless 13. Touch 14. Conservation 15. Affirm 16. Inductive 17. Merciless 18. Snoop 19. Wile 20. Loyalty

Time

The end of a millennium is a mark in time
When we pause to catch our breath
We stop to inspect the harvest of our lives that
We will take over to the zone of the Marshal
One licks his wounds of insanity as a
Requisite and Cathartic means to salvation
The harsh reality between good and evil
Continues to clash as we damn the stick of guidance
Will this new era in time pad out for us
Or will we watch the world flush down the drain
I can only hope that a new world will
Splay before us with hope and love

Challenge Words ~ Poem #2

1. millennium 2. harvest 3. Cathartic 4. Requisite 5. insanity 6. Marshal 7. salvation 8. reality 9. clash 10. splay 11, breath 12. wounds 13. pad 14. mark 15. salvation 16. flush 17. catch 18. inspect 19. era 20. zone

Resurrection

The steady rhythm of the motion
Of the train going downhill
Filled a spot of my impecunious heart
With a piquancy that left a chill
I knew that the devilish Red Sultan
Was trying to consummate my confession
By overmastering my mysticism and
Making a pitch to join his procession
He had already taken me out of circulation
I had to take a stand to retrieve my entitlement
A special fight to enrich and restore my soul
The costly kind that will bring enlightenment

Challenge Words ~ Poem #3

1. sultan 2. rhythm 3. train 4. impecunious 5. piquancy 6. choll 7. consummate 8. confession 9. mysticism 10. pitch 11. procession 12. circulation 13. entitlement 14. enlightenment 15. enrich 16. retrieve 17. motion 18. kind 19. overmastering 20. stand

Renewal

The teenage marriage ended soon
Beneath an ornamental radial moon
She fondled her crocheted dress
Which the muddled weather made a mess
He ran off to the south carrying his crossbow
His phytophagous appetite made him go
The old omelet on the plate began to ferment
As she read the disenchanted letter he sent
She stared and tried to understand his ignorance
And to summarize their problems at a glance
She must erase the principal memories of him
And start her life all over again
No one is given a quota of love
We must grab it from the stars above

Challenge Words ~ Poem #4

1. tennage 2. ornamental 3. radial 4. mess 5. omelet 6. ferment 7. appetite 8. muddled 9. crochet 10. quota 11. disenchanted 12. ignorance 13. erase 14. crossbow 15. weather 16. phytophagous 17. summarize 18. moon 19. glance 20. grab

School Poems

Band Memories

When I was a kid in high school
I was in the Raider Marching Band
I'd blow real hard on my saxophone
When the majorette lowered her hand

We'd rise real early each morning
To practice our flashy routines
If only I could learn to count
And not bump into the tambourines

Our uniforms were old as the hills
In school colors of gold and blue
We sold millions of candy bars over
The years, hoping to buy some new

But wear those uniforms we did
With pride as we belted out a tune
And it was a very sad day when
We hung up those threads in June

I remember my time in marching band
And hold memories close to my heart
And every time I hear the big bass drum
I get chills and tears may start

So march and play on young musicians
Send your tunes out over the land
For when you are old, like I am,
You'll remember the marching band

School Marm

I still hear the voices on the playground
And the bouncing of a basketball
I hear the tap tap tap of a jump rope
I smell the fresh air of the Fall

I hear the rustling of the papers
I love the smell of a brand new book
I see the smiles the children get
When the teacher gives a special look

I hear the crackling of the speaker
As daily announcements are read
The children aren't paying attention
They won't remember what's been said

I hear the rumble of the school bus
As it comes slowly down the road
Full of laughing and happy children
It stops by the school to unload

I taught sweet young children
For just a few short years
When I think back upon those times
My eyes swell up with tears

My days of teaching are over
Remembering children of every kind
And when I pass a school yard
Those memories flood my mind

Day Care Teacher

She tightened the buckle on my skate
Made sure my helmet was on good and tight
She watched me learn to skate today
So I could show mom and dad tonight

Up and down the sidewalk
I glided as an Olympic star
Performing in front of my favorite judge
I didn't dare go too far

Live for today, little child
For some day that will all end
They'll tell you she is not good for you
You can no longer be her friend

A child does not understand
Why the woman who brought her joy
Has to be treated differently
Then cast out like an old used toy

Let's all become like children
And see all people as the same
Never allowing others
To put our friends to shame

The Sub

Strange faces look up at me
Just waiting to hear what I'll say
Wondering what their teacher left
With me to give them today

The seconds tick by so slowly
And anxious eye peeks to see
Will I have time to finish this
Or will I have to quit and let it be

A restless foot is tapping
As pages are turned one by one
A pencil scratches across the line
Until the grueling task is done

The students are restless as the time
Draws near for the final bell to ring
And to think of what joy and happiness
Is brought by that one small thing

The lights above me are buzzing
A locker door slams in the hall
Children are shouting on the playground
Oh gosh, how I miss it all

THE TEACHER'S DESK

An old worn desk pad sits atop,
the pencils have broken lead.
There's no fancy tissue box for runny noses,
a roll of toilet paper instead.

Textbooks are aligned for every class,
and papers are stacked so high.
Attendance sheets, hall passes and note
pads are there, anything to get by.

Tests to give and papers to grade are waiting
from a very long and tiring day.
I guess it's time to go home now,
because everything is put away.

Ode to a School Bus Driver

I heard the sound and then looked up
Just in time to see
The big yellow bus go on by which
Brings memories back to me

I think about the driver there
That takes students to and fro
He talks to them and treats them well
As he is always on the go

Every day is different for him
Although each day is still the same
He knows each child's precious face
And tries hard to remember each name

He picks them up and takes them home
He's always so prompt and on time
The students are there with time to spare
To hear that old school bell chime

From kindergarten through twelfth grade
To ride the bus is a thrill
The kids all know and love him
They'll remember him forever, yes they will.

Rob

Deep,
So deep in the dark water of the river,
The purple fish, with his strong body,
Swims against the current.
The youth, too smart for schools,
Wants to venture out and learn all about the world.
His eyes appear as a fish much older and wiser.
But, his face is that of a child.
He dreams.
He hopes.
He wants.
What does this purple fish want?
Freedom?
Wealth?
He has both.
Love?
I cannot give him love –
Only my friendship.
I can be his teacher and his friend.
But, what can I teach him?
He must have the experiences of life alone.
I cannot teach him these things.
One day he will be a great purple fish,
And he will have forgotten me.
Good luck my young friend.
I will miss you.

For "Our Kids"

My heart is breaking
And I have to wipe away a tear
Because it's the same news
It seems I hear every year!

Another young child
Is being laid to rest today
Because of a senseless accident
Along a country roadway.

How many friends must be taken?
How many lives must be lost?
How many bones must be broken?
Who really bears the cost?

We know our roads are narrow
With many a hill and turn.
Driving is a privilege
And is something we must earn.

Our roads are crossed by animals.
And with farmers we must share.
And if you are five minutes late
Who is really going to care?

Stop and think of ones so dear
Of David, Michelle, Bryan, Chance,
Eric, Felisha, and Jessica, too.
Please slow down, dear friends,
So it doesn't happen to you.

Deep Thoughts

The Bridge

The raging waters rush by, cleansing the world around
Taking away sad memories, and crushing them down
The bridges are crumbling, rotten with decay
But, the one we are building now is here to stay
In my dreams I hold you close and touch your face
You look at me and kiss on that tender place
We met through pictures, letters and chat
But I feel there is much more than that
My heart is full, the words cannot flow
What I feel, I still cannot show
The bridge is there waiting for you and me
To cross together to see what will be

Lost Son

They said he was a bad boy
They treated him with spite
It isn't any wonder then
Why he stayed out late each night

They told him to do his homework
They yelled at him about his chores
The only time he could block it out
Is when he was out of doors.

They pushed him to the limit
Then they pushed a little more
Did they want him to be perfect?
Is that what they were striving for?

A boy can only do so much
When he is learning how to fly
But if nothing is ever good enough
Why should he even try?

Two parents grieve by a graveside
No words are being said
Because their son finally "did it right"
When he put a pistol to his head.

Before he died the last thing he did
Was to write a very short note
"Mom, Dad, I tried my best"
And that was all he wrote.

The Letter

The soldier lay upon his bunk waiting for his orders for the day
Holding the letter in his hand from his young son far away.

"Dear daddy", it said "I met some new friends today.
We have so much fun at school and we love to laugh and play.
My friend Jamal likes sports and his hair is real curly and black.
Then there's Sky who has long dark braids down his back.

Petrov is blonde, dad, he looks like you and me
And Miguel is so funny even though he cannot see.
We made a club, dad, and call ourselves the Rad High Fives
We promise to be friends, dad, for all the rest of our lives.

Akiko wanted to join our club and play with all our toys
Girls are icky, aren't they, dad. Our club is just for boys."
The soldier put the letter down with tears running down his face.
How will he ever explain to his son what he is doing is this
horrible place.

Why can't we all be like children and see others with innocent
eyes.
We'd look upon our differences with a respect that never dies.

Feelings of 9-11

The television is on
No sound is heard
The newsmen there
Can find no word

The horrible image
Really says it all
Airplanes crashed into
The towers so tall

I sit in amazement
This sight is so bad
People crying and grieving
Oh my, it's so sad

It's been quite some time
But we have not forgotten
Smoke still billows
Like soft balls of cotton

At first we were in school
And we cried many tears
We vowed to seek justice
If it takes many years

God bless America
The home of the brave
This land of the free
We'll fight hard to save

Survivor

He sat at his desk
It was a regular day
When an explosion was heard
And the building began to sway

Looking out his window
All he could see was smoke
And when he got up
He began to choke

The lights were flickering
And finally went out
As he ran to the stairwell
He could hear people shout

He ran down the stairs
First one flight then another
All he could think about
Was getting home to his mother

The building was shaking
As he stepped from each stair
Silently hoping and praying
That the next would be there

Steel beams were crying
The walls began to sway
Just three steps later
The floor gave away

He fell a short ways
Fighting concrete and steel
Landing in darkened rubble
Only fear could he feel

The gash on his head gave him no pain
He couldn't feel his legs
"Oh God, don't let me die!"
This lonely man did beg

"Not today, my son," God said
"You have much more to do"
Just then he saw a fireman's smile
And cried, "I'm so glad to see you"

His wounds are healed now
Only nightmarish memories stay
And when he gets scared
He bows his head to pray

Praying for the men and women
Who went into the mob
Saying, "Aw, 'twas nothing,
Just doing our job"

My Special Candle

There are so many candles
That burn so very bright
And put all those candles together
We can light up the dark of night

Some are for young soldiers
To guide them home again
Some are for friends and family
To keep them free from pain

Dear Lord. I have one of those candles
For a soldier, friends and family, too
Can you watch over them, please?
I know you have lots to do.

For me I ask for nothing
I have great blessings galore
I thank you for each one, Dear Lord
And need nothing more

So keep an eye on my candle
Each morning at its start
And at night when I blow it out
The light's still lit in my heart

Wesley's Candle

I light a candle every day
And say a little prayer
Asking God to keep you safe
While you are over there.

The candle sits a top a shelf
Its light is not very bright
But when it is dark and eerie out
It let's off a wonderful light

A soft yet glowing light
That makes one feel so warm
Reminding God each time He sees
To keep you safe from harm

This candle will burn for you
My friend; each and every day
And prayers will be said, too
Until you come home to stay

Father and Son

For nine months a child grows
inside the tummy of a mother
But the love for this child
grows inside the heart of another

She nurtures the baby, he cares for her,
their love grows day by day
And on that very special day he cuts the cord
in his special gentle way

He looks at his son with so much pride
that he cannot help but cry
The tiny little person is a part of him,
a gift given from the sky

The Father holds the tiny babe
in his big strong callused hand
This child will want for nothing;
Dad will do all that he can

You will never know the joy
he feels until you are the one
Who holds a newborn babe,
the child you call son.

My Special Boys

All I ever wanted that you have someone special in your life
And of course I was hoping she would be a very pretty wife
So you could be happy just like my husband and me
And then you could have your own sweet family

But I look into your eyes; they seem so dark and sad
Are you hiding something? Is it something bad?
You're the kindest, sweetest guy, good looking, too.
Nothing could be so wrong. Everything is perfect with you.

Tell me now. Take the load off, please.
Whatever is bothering you will put your heart at ease.
No matter what you did, or what you are
We'll still love you, know that by far.

Instead of a wife, I'll wish for someone who'll care
Who'll hold you close and stroke your hair
As long as you are happy with yourself everyday
It doesn't matter to me 'cause I'll love you anyway.

Not My Son!

What are you saying?
You're a mean, ornery brat!
Why are you so cruel!
What'd I do to deserve that!

Was it my all fault
You turned out this way?
Could I have done something different
So you wouldn't be gay?

My son looked at me
With sad downturned eyes
He still wants my love
But he can't apologize

I'm sorry son
Don't go away
There's a place in my heart
You can always stay

A place in our home
You'll be welcome, too
I can't imagine my life
Living without my son like you.

Friends & Family

Michael

A child cries in a distant world
There is silence all around
Her mother lies so cold and still
Next to her on the ground

A man comes and picks her up
He holds her with one arm
He speaks so soft and gentle now
Protecting her from any harm

She feels so free and safe now
As she looks into his face
He's running now through mud and weeds
Away from that horrible place

The shots ring out so loud, so fierce
They are heard across the land
This isn't how it was supposed to be
It's not the way it was planned

A child cries in a distant world
There is silence all around
A young soldier lies so cold and still
Next to her on the ground

Aunt Pat

She's short and sweet and so rotund
She's got a heart as big as the sea
She's loud and says just what she thinks
And she's become like a mother to me

She tells you just how things should be
She never pulls any punches
She thinks things through carefully
Before playing upon her hunches

I remember on my wedding day
She sat proud in the front row
Her tears flowed freely from start to end
She let her emotions show

Although she comes through really tough
And sometimes growls like a bear
My Aunt Pat is the sweetest gal
And I'm thankful she's always there

JOYce

For a high school dance with a Cookie Monster
She made me look pretty & fixed up my hair
Even years before that I looked up to her
She was like a big sister, who was always there

When mom was sick I spent weeks with them
We slept in big feather beds
She'd tell us scary stories of the golden arm
And sneak up and ruffle our heads.

Or tell us about the time
When the neighbor's gorilla got loose
Or when I fell off the old horse Lady and
Landed right in the poops.

We aren't really close but she's always been special
She's one of the nicest people you'll ever meet
She got married to Steve, had two good looking sons
Is a hard working gal and is very sweet

She's got an inner beauty
That makes you smile and makes you feel good inside.
She is a grown up daughter of Louise and Ralph,
One of the middle girls of the Dieker Tribe

Why do bad things happen to good people?
A better person you will never find right here.
She has suffered through illness, lost a son,
her home to a fire and her husband so dear.

They say if it does not kill us it makes us stronger
Well I am here to tell you she is strong
With friends and family and God around her
She still stands among us all the days long.

Some days she may not show it
Some days she may not have it to share
But those day just call on your cousin and friend
Because I will have that JOY for you, because I care.

Erin

I remember sitting in the waiting room
Waiting with my mom and dad
Waiting for a child to be born
It was the longest day we ever had

The nurse came in all smiles
And said we had a girl
We were so excited
Our minds were in a whirl

That little girl is so cute
Smiling and laughing as she plays
She grew so tall and beautiful
Throughout many many days

She tried to be a dancer
But cried during her debut
She tried many different things
Always wanting something new

That little girl is all grown up
She even drives a car
She does so well in school
I know that she will go far

I regret the day that she leaves us
And goes off on her own
I hope she'll remember Aunt Becky
Who'll be waiting by the phone

Someday she will marry
And we'll be waiting to hear
If she had a baby boy
Or a daughter to hold dear

Brian

After what seemed many days
We were told she had a boy
A son, a nephew was born today
He brought us so much joy

Grandma called him Bubba
'cause he was so short and stout
And when he talked you'd better listen close
As he told you what it's all about

He loves to play baseball
He hits an occasional home run
He loves the game of soccer
And golf is so much fun

He didn't care much for football
He didn't like the pain
And he gets so unhappy
Whenever it would rain

He does so well in school
And is such a real nice guy
That I know that someday
He'll reach his dreams in the sky

I would be proud to call him "son"
But he's just a nephew to me
But more than that he is my friend
And friends we'll always be

Stan

When he was little
And had nothing to do
He'd crawl in the cabinets
And get out a pot or two

He used those pots
Just like a set of drums
And drove us all batty
With his rum-a-tum-tums

He used some spoons as drumsticks
He really had a good beat
And when he was a little older
He got a real fancy set with a seat

He'd play for hours in his room
With music blasting in his head
He kept the beat to all the songs
From Grand Funk to the Greatful Dead

He is now a professional drummer
Playing in a local band
And when people listen to him play
They tap their feet and clap their hands

Although he drove me crazy
When he was just a kid
I am glad to say he's my brother
And I am proud of all he did

But two of his best accomplishments
The best things that he's ever had
Are my wonderful niece and nephew
The kids that call him Dad

Dear Mother

I never really knew you
But a part of you am I
When we met that first time
All I did was cry

I never really knew you
But without you I'd not be
You gave me birth than gave me away
And with that, you set me free

I never really knew you
What your life was like before
All I know is this true fact
You wanted to give me more

I never really knew you
Or why you gave me away
Life would have been so different
If you'd only let me stay

I never really knew you
For this I am very sad
But thank you for giving me life
For this I am very glad

Someday I will get to know you
When we meet in Heaven above
When all will be forgiven
And we share a special love

With love and caring now
We are here to set you free
May you find peace and freedom
Floating over the sea

Karen

Words cannot express
How grateful that I feel
To finally have a sister
Not make believe but real

When I look at you
It's like looking in a mirror
Our times we'll spend together
I'll always hold dear

Though many years have passed
We didn't know each other from the start
There'll always be a special place for you
Deep down inside my heart

I always felt there was someone
To tell my special secrets to
I'm so glad I found that someone
And guess what! It's you!

Daddy

Memories of a lifelong past
Continue living in his mind
The love he shared, the wife he had
So sweet, so gentle, so kind

His childhood memories are so vivid,
So sharp and so clear
But he can no longer remember
That she left this world last year

He talks to others of the woman
He loved and knew as Ruth
It is hard for us to remind him
Of the sad and troubling truth

He knows his life has changed
It will never be the same
Yet he misses her and wants her near
He calls others by her name

The loneliness engulfs his spirit
His heart is so sad
I pray there is something I can do
Because he is my dad

For My Mom

Mom

Her hands were gnarled from years of toil
The map of life etched across her face
She tucked me in bed till I was grown
And kissed me on that tender place

A bad word for no one did she have
Even though many had done her wrong
Always a kind word, a helping hand
Were given her whole life long

In the garden she could always be found
Tending to seedlings breaking the ground
Later in the fall when the plants did mature
She'd put those fruits in jars for the future

She might have been frugal, but never so tight
I remember her scolding "turn off that light"
She'd stretch a dollar and make it go around
She'd give of herself without making a sound

She's gone now and I miss her so much
To hear her voice or feel her touch
Still to this day I pick up the phone
Then realizing she's gone, I'm so alone

This woman, so beautiful and kind,
Wanted me when there was no other
I miss her so, but am proud to say
This woman was my mother.

Oh, Mom

Growing up in the '50's was so very different
Life was so slow, so safe and so very sweet.
No locked doors, good books, both parents at home
And on hot nights out in the yard we'd sleep.

Dad went to work every day of the week
And Mom doled out the chores
And when those were done and rooms were clean
We'd play all day out of doors.

When I was tall enough I'd help Mom
Hang the clothes out on the line
Then helped to fold them all and put
Away my brother's clothes and mine.

On Sundays we would get to church early
Mom with her crystal beads and her eyes bowed low
She spoke silently as her fingers moved over them
She was praying for us, you know.

No matter where we were or where we went
I always wanted to hold Mom's hand in mine
She never pulled away or said she had no time
It was our way of showing our love, our special sign.

Mom was ill for many years
Not a fatal disease but one with pain
She suffered a lot but worked right through it
Continuing to smile, and never complain

She stood behind me and pushed me on
Bragging about my accomplishments and deeds
Without her I would have been nothing
Because she saw and fulfilled all my needs

How am I going to make it without her?
Who is going to take care of me?
For I am nothing without her
She was the best part of me.

Who's going to take care of me?

"Who's going to take care of me?" I cried.
My mother is no longer alive
"Who's going to take care of me?" I cried.
I'm only a bit older than 45.

"Who's going to take care of me?" I wept.
They're putting my mother in the ground.
. "Who's going to take care of me?" I wept..
I screamed but there was no sound.

"Who's going to take care of me?" I sobbed.
Everyone is leaving by two or three.
"Who's going to take care of me?" I sobbed..
I'm going home with just me.

"Who's going to take care of me?" I sighed
They've just ripped out my heart.
"Who's going to take care of me?" I sighed.
No one. My dying is beginning to start.

Sniff

Life goes on
What is life?
Sleep happens
What is sleep?
Television flickers
The channels changing
What am I watching?
Bed? What is a bed?

Holidays come and go
Halloween ~ Boo Who
Thanksgiving ~ for what?
Christmas ~ Ho Ho Ha Ha
Happy Freaking New Year

Her smell is gone
A blouse ~ her scarf
Her smell is gone
Rummage through another bag
Another dress
Another shirt
I can't remember her smell
Tears flowing
I hold her shirt to my face
It's damp
I smell her…
I smell her!
I embrace the shirt
Tears flow
I sleep

Hey Mom

Hey Mom did you hear that? It's up in the tree.
A little wren announcing the birth of her babies three
Oh listen, Mom, a robin singing her beautiful song
And the whippoorwill sings all night long

Oh Mom, look at this. The blooms on the trees are big and bright
Get out the sheets. They say it is going to frost tonight.
The tulips and iris are pretty on stalks so tall
I think your roses are the prettiest of all

Oh Momma, I saw that tear when Erin was put in your arms
You'd give your life to keep her safe from all world harms
When Brian was born you called him Bubba 'cause he was short and loud
They're both grown up now, Mom. You'd be so proud

Mom, I finally met a guy I love. He wouldn't meet your goals I know
He's divorced, not once but twice and he's not even Catholic, so…
He's kind, and loving. I know you'd like him, I really do.
He'd answer all your questions, Mom, and very honestly, too.

You were at our wedding smiling down, a special honor to you was said
Pictures of you and Matt's mom were on the altar just below the Head
To the reception you followed and sat upon our table
I know you would have danced with us if you had been able

Did you hear that Mom? Your words coming out of my mouth
I guess I did listen to you back then when we lived just south
Oh Mom I still miss you so much that it hurts in my heart
It seems you were here just yesterday that we've been apart

Momma, Where are you?

Momma! Momma! Momma, where are you?
I don't see you. Have I gone blind?
Momma, are you here? I can't feel you.
Take my hand if you'd be so kind.

Momma! Momma! Momma, where are you?
Are you outside working in the yard?
Momma, I'm looking all over ~ even
In the garden ~ oh this is so hard.

Momma! Momma! Momma, where are you?
Did you leave without me ~ you wouldn't dare.
Momma, please come out of hiding now
You are giving me quite a scare.

Momma! Momma! Momma, where are you?
Did you take a long walk down by the creek?
Momma, why didn't you take me along?
Did you wear those old shoes that leak?

Momma! Momma! Momma, where are you?
Did Dad take you away never to come back?
Momma, were you hurt real bad, did you cry?
All I have now is all your things in a sack.

Momma! Momma! Momma, where are you?
No, it can't be! They tell me that you died.
Momma, please tell me that it isn't so,
Tell me that you are ok and that they have lied.

Momma! Momma! Momma, I know where you are.
You're in Heaven sitting between Jesus and your Dad.
Momma, I will miss you forever with sadness
But smile at the wonderful memories we had.

I'm Trying My Best

A new day dawns but I don't see the sun
It's just another morning
I get up and maybe get dressed
It's just another day of mourning

I always remember to thank God
For the many gifts from above
But my heart feels so empty
Is there no love?

My loving husband sleeps
Quietly next to me
Between us curled up tightly
Is our sweet little Doogie

Our house is cozy and comfortable
We don't need any more
There are no wolves
Howling at our door

We have to do more than being good
That's what the preachers say
If you want to be at God's side
Come that wonderful judgment day

I work at it and try so hard to be good
Sometimes it makes me cry
Those words scare me sometimes
And I am so afraid to die

You know Mom, if I am not saved
And my faith and feelings are not true
I will not go to heaven and that means
I will never again be with you

One More Day

I used to complain every Saturday when you'd call
And you wanted me to roll up your hair
I'd get the brown wash out color on my fingers, too
You have no idea how much I wish you were there

I remember sneaking into the house after Dad had gotten up
I would go quietly to your room and slip into bed with you
You'd squeal because I was cold but you never pushed me away
And we'd cuddle; you'd kiss my head and ask me what's new

I always told the truth, you knew if I was lying ~
You knew since I was young ~ so I never even tried
We'd talk of good things and bad, and have a few good laughs
You knew things from years long ago that I tried to hide

Mom, you gave me all the love you had
You gave me everything you had and then lots more
You sacrificed and went without so I had what I wanted
You know you spoiled me rotten to the core

I guess I always assumed you would be around
I figured you would be here until I was real old
People are living to the century mark now
But that's not the way your story was to be told

When they took you in to set your arm you grumbled
I told you it beat the alternative of Duker & Haugh
Never in a million years would I have believed that
In just 2 days we would be holding a vigil in the hall

People waited and prayed for more than ten hours
They were coming and going and 65 came through
There were sisters, brothers, nieces and nephews
As well as Dad, Stan and I were there with you

We followed your wishes and pulled the plug
It was the hardest thing I ever had to do
We knew you didn't want to live like that
Oh my God, how I am missing you

The School House is Gone

Guess what Mom. You're never going to believe it.
I'll tell you a story; I hope I don't bring you tears.
Remember the school house that became our home
The gentleman's farm with memories of 40 years?

A guy bought it who who was a real slob
He came to live there shortly after you moved to town
He didn't take care of it and let the grass grow high
Things got so bad that the back wall started to fall down

Now our school house is gone, the bulldozers came
First the barns then the house came down brick by brick
The memories tumbled each time the wrecking ball hit
I picked up some dust and held it tightly; I had to make it stick

It looked so strange and empty for a time
The garage and the mailbox were the only things that stand
The a new house was built, small and modern
Some of our trees were left and they leveled out the land

Remember the trees, Mom? Our Arbor Day Maples in the front yard
The Red Delicious apple tree you planted for me by the gate
And the tiny sprout of a Blue Spruce you smuggled from
Canada in your purse is now so full, tall and straight

It does look nice now compared to a while ago
The neighbors all like it and say it looks fine
I must admit it does look better but
It will never look as good as it did in our time

There are no cows laying in the green grass of the pasture
There is no Dalmatian resting against their warm hide
The lawn is not perfectly groomed around the white fences
And no one spent more time in the garden on the side

The flowers were neatly weeded and colors were glorious
Each season gave praise with tulips, roses and mums
Even the garden gave more than enough vegetables
To put away for all of us and friends when winter comes

With nothing but dirt left with the grass scraped away
No shape of a garden ~ no sign of orchard trees
No blooming flowers, not even a sign of a bed is left
It's only in my heart that I will hold on to these memories.

Did I make you cry, Mom? Or did I bring back good thoughts?
Do you have a flower garden in Heaven? Do you have trees?
Did you plant some tomatoes or smuggle a Blue Spruce with you?
Or maybe you planted another Red Delicious Apple tree for me.

For Matt

The Search

A long time ago in a time far away
I looked for a place where I could stay
'Twas to be in the country where I could run free
With the wind in my hair and my shadow chasing me
The sun will shine on my face so warm
Sparkling in the sky like a golden charm

I looked so long and hard for such a place
I prayed to be blessed with such holy grace
I moved to a house in the country, you see
With my Dalmatian, Max, and my cat, PurrC
The land was so beautiful, so open and free
But, something was missing. What could it be?

The sun went down each night in a sea of red
The breezes blew cool between the barn and the shed
The trees in summer had leaves so puffy and green
And the Autumn brought colors like you have never seen
This was the place I had looked for so long
But, I still wasn't happy. What could be wrong?

Three years we have lived here, just me and my pets
I'll settle for this because it's the best that it gets
Not true! Not true! Cried a voice from above
The only thing missing here is a thing called love
Where can I find love? Where can it be?
When the time is right, you'll surely see

My house in the country became a home one day
It happened when you walked through the door to stay
No longer will I feel lonely in the farm on the hill
And I will cuddle with you when the winds blow a chill
I didn't need to look so far or so wide
I just look in your eyes and see the love deep inside

The Deer

She stands there so all alone
by the dark deserted country road.
The wind and rain are stronger now,
she shivers in the cold.

Her eyes try to pierce the darkness
to see what lies ahead.
She is afraid to move forward;
so she stands very still instead.

The rain has stopped and the
clouds have been pushed away.
She sees the moon now trying
to guide her along the right way.

"Oh thank you, Mr. Moon, my friend"
she cries into the night.
"I thought I was all alone here,
but you have given back my sight."

Cautiously, but full of hope,
she takes that first brave step.
The moon has washed away her fears
that the cold harsh darkness kept

First Glance

The plane ride was bumpy
I arrived very late
I looked around in horror
Because I didn't see my date

It was only a couple minutes
But it seemed it was for hours
Before he came around the corner
Behind a big bouquet of flowers

I looked at him, he looked at me
We smiled when our loving eyes met
If I knew it was going to be this good
I wouldn't have needed the jet

That first kiss was gentle
Not passionate, but rather sweet
It was at that moment I knew
That we were destined to meet

We knew from the start
We would be together for life
And now I am happy to say
That I am his loving wife

You are loved

If I were a robin
Living in a distant tree
I'd fly toward you in a hurry
Just so I could see
You

Many times I have thought if
You only knew how much I care
Wanting to be in your town,
Your state, or just any where
You are

Sometimes I wonder what
I should do so you will know
Little things to remind you
Just little things to show
You are loved

Transplant

He came from the big city
And moved to my small town
The peace and the quiet here
Would never bring him down

He heard coyotes cry
In the middle of the night
It was a peaceful sound
Never causing him fright

He was used to the sounds
Of the sirens that screamed
Not to mention the air which
Was as thick as soup it seemed

But here in the country
The air seems so light
Even the smells from the barnyard
Gave him some delight

He's a country boy now
And life is so good
He's taking life easy
Just as he should

Night

The wind whistles through the cracks of the old farmhouse
That sits upon the hill
The moon is bright but the night is cold
There seems to be a chill

The coyotes howl from distant woods
The cows are asleep and safe from harm
The cat curls up upon my lap
We are all cozy and warm

So why is the night so scary
When all is safe and sound
Maybe because I am all alone
Away from the love I found

The miles between us are many
But the moon we share is the same
I look up at the star filled sky
And gently whisper his name

The night is not so scary now
I feel all warm inside
I remember times together
When we slept side by side

I'll go to bed and sleep peaceful now
All cuddly warm, safe and sound
I'll dream of him and the memories we made
And of the precious man I found

For My Husband

Upon my pillow there lies a rose
the aroma of it fills my nose

Upon his chest I lay my head
every night when we go to bed

Upon my heart he casts his spell
how much I love him, I cannot tell

Upon our lives God always smiles
and helps us through many miles

The Circle

A circle has no beginning
And it also has no end.
It's been written about so often,
Time and time again.

A circle is an endless thing
Whether it's oval or it's round
It symbolizes many precious things
Like a special love that is found.

Two circles entwined together
Will forever be unbroken;
They symbolize a life long love
And vows that have been spoken.

The circle of gold upon my hand
Is the circle I hold most dear.
It was given to me by the one I love
To remind me he will always be near

My Wedding Day

The rain came down in buckets
On this, my special day
I prayed so much for sunshine
Oh, well, what can I say?

The church was full of people
All waiting so patiently
Can you believe it!
They were waiting just for me!

Finally the music began
The attendants walked up the aisle
Standing there at my father's side
It seemed as long as a mile

The sea of faces turned my way
I can not tell you who was there
For standing at the altar
Was the one for which I cared

He stood there waiting, straight and tall
His face showed pride and fear
A tiny smile broke his lips
I had to choke back a tear

The pastor began the service
With a short sweet prayer about love
By exchanging our vows we became one
As our Mothers watched from above

"Oh Mom, I know you'd love him,
He's so handsome, gentle and kind
Dad thinks he's pretty special, too"
I'm so glad to say he is mine.

We left the church and took a carriage ride
Around the town and through the park
After saying good-bye to all our friends
We went on a riverboat at dark

My special day began with rain
It ended that way, too
Bur, it was the best day of my entire life
Because we started our lives brand new

Fun Stuff

New Year's Resolution

The stockings were put away
With such loving care
We all were certain that
Santa had been there

Not to mention Aunt Bess,
Uncle Bob and their little tot
That turkey we stuffed and the
Yams we baked sure hit the spot

New Year's Eve bubbly
Tickled more than my nose
Everything is swollen
From my head to my toes.

Jenny Craig, Nutrisystem,
Diet Center, Curves and TOPS
I'll go to them all before
Each of my buttons pops

I will lose weight
I promise this year
I will be strong
I have no fear

I'll stretch every morning
As soon as I wake up
But first I need coffee,
Please pass me a cup

I'll walk after lunch
I won't go very far at first
I made it to the Fast Stop
Need a Pepsi to quench my thirst.

I'll do my exercises each night
I'll fix healthy meals every day
And when I go out to dinner sometime
I'll pass up that yummy dessert tray.

By the time next year rolls around
I hope to be a little lighter
Because if I keep going the way I am
My clothes will just keep getting tighter

My Car

It sits in the garage at the ready
Waiting for me to go
In any kind of nasty weather
Wind, rain, fog or snow

The tires are worn
There are dents in the door
But I am sure that I can still get
At least a hundred thousand more

The mud is caked around the wheels
The windows are such a blur
For what little attention I give to it
It's a darn good car for sure

I give it gas once a week
Being sure to fill the tank
It's old, it runs, it belongs to me
And never more to the bank

Bad Habits

Do you like to pick your nose?
Do you wipe it on your clothes?
Do you wipe it on a chair?
Or do you flick it in the air?
Do you eat it like your brother
Just to hear the screams of mother?

Do you like to scratch your butt?
Or pick the scab off a day old cut?
Do you fart when in a crowd?
Oh my goodness, not too loud.
Or do you leave a smelly hiss,
Then blame it on your little sis?
Or lying in bed, you just can't wait
To pull the sheet up over your mate?

When in church do you like to nap
Until the preacher starts to tap?
Or have you ever laughed so hard
That you almost wet your garb?
Have you belched real loud after dinner?
Are these the acts of a normal sinner?
I hear the groans and giggles from you
But we've all done it; yes, you, too.

Through His Eyes

A picture is worth a thousand words
It's been said many times before
And to put sunsets and star filled skies
Into words is a mighty chore

But to catch a bird in winged flight
Or soft rays through full branched trees
Is the task of love, a work of art
When a photographer shares what he sees

Me, A Writer?

Why is it today I can write so much
The words just seem to come
When yesterday I stared at an empty page
And I felt really, really dumb

The words seem to come so freely today
As the ink flows out of my pen
I'm on a roll. What should I do?
Maybe write something for my friend

Let's see, rose are red
And violets are blue
Hmmm, all I can think of is
I love you

The block is back, the words are stuck
My mind seems to be getting tighter
But this is a poem that I just wrote
My Gosh! I must be a writer.

Becky Coelho is from a mid-size city on the Mississippi River in west central Illinois. She enjoys meeting people as well as watching them. Her poems are about people she knows and loves, about her life as a school teacher and the beauty of nature when she lived on a small farm. There is a section of poems written after her mother's death when she was deep depression. But not to fear, meeting and falling in love with her husband brought her back to this world and there are special poems for him, too. Becky also has a sense of humor and that is shown in some of her verses.

Becky enjoys writing stories as well as poetry and thanks her English teachers throughout her school days for giving her the joy of writing.

She lives with her husband, Matt and their three dogs. She is very busy with several volunteer organizations including leading an Adaptive Water Exercise Class for the Red Cross and being an Asst. Coach for Special Olympics.

www.ingramcontent.com/pod-product-compliance
Ingram Content Group UK Ltd.
Pitfield, Milton Keynes, MK11 3LW, UK
UKHW041924190726
13854UKWH00003B/1433